This Book Belongs to:

_____

_____

_____

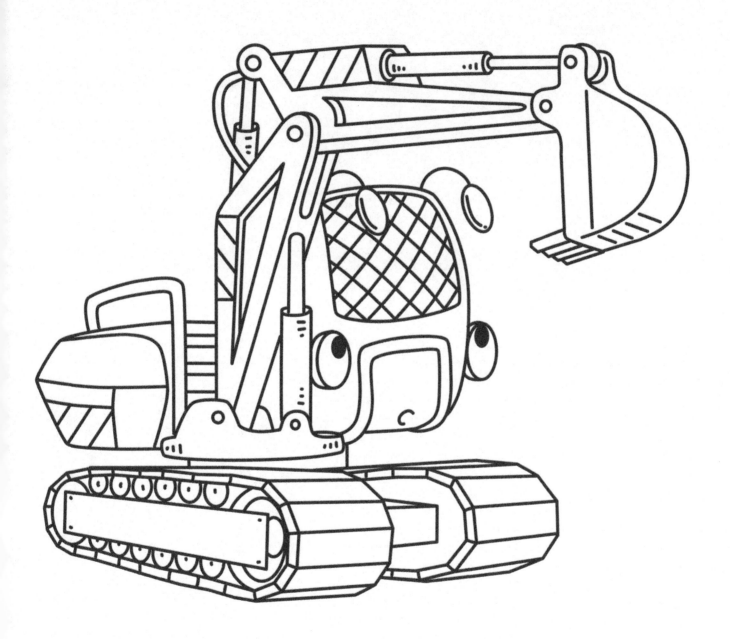

Find One of a Kind

Find 10 Differences

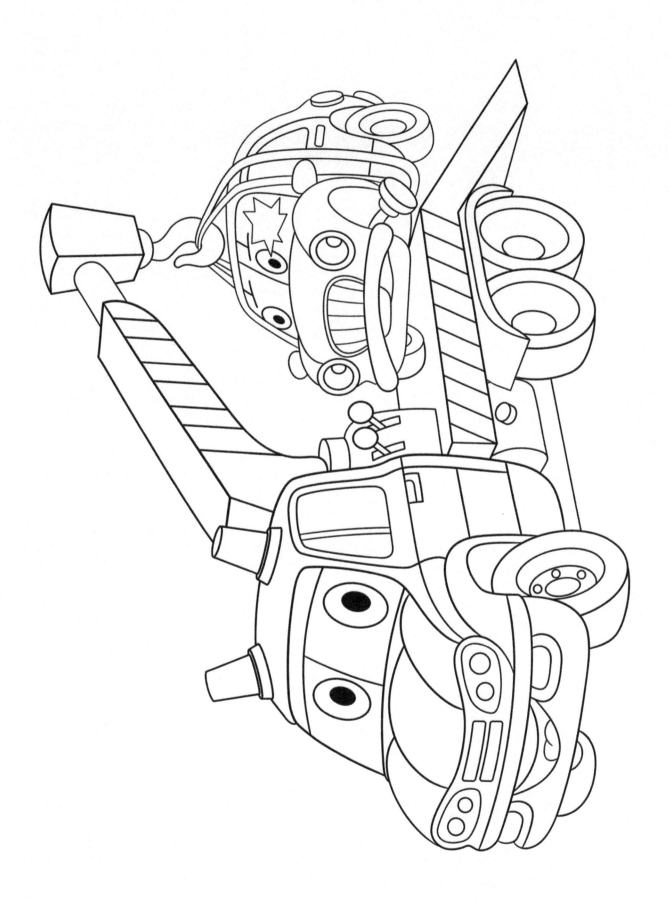

Copy the
Picture

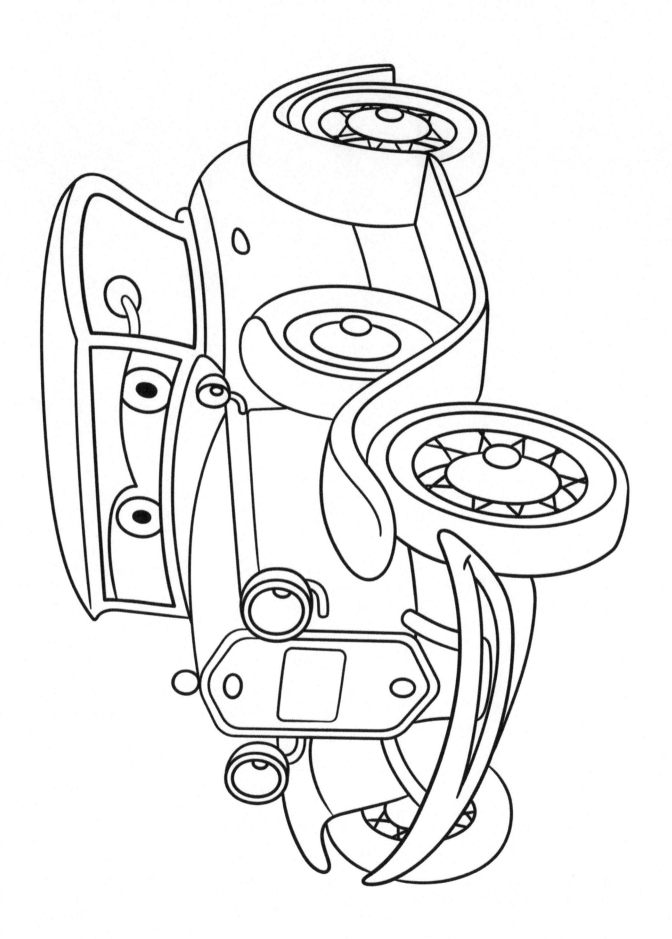

Find 6 Differences

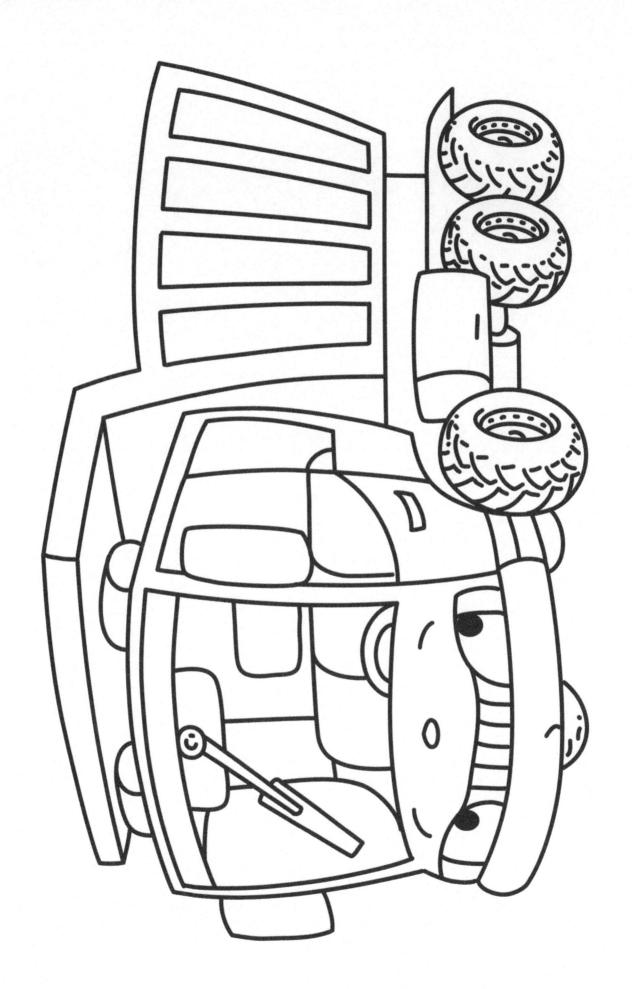

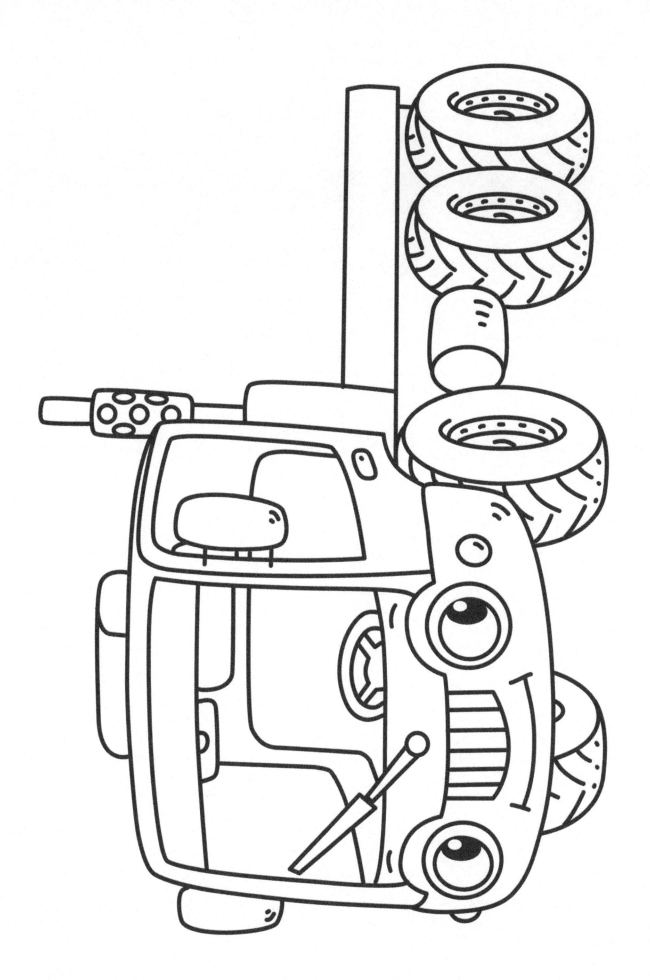

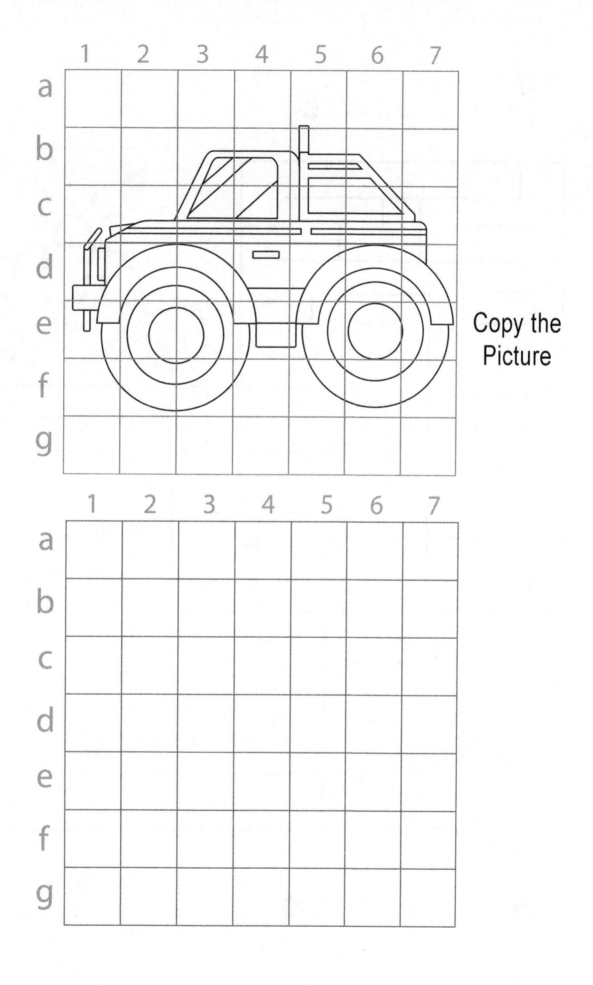

Copy the
Picture

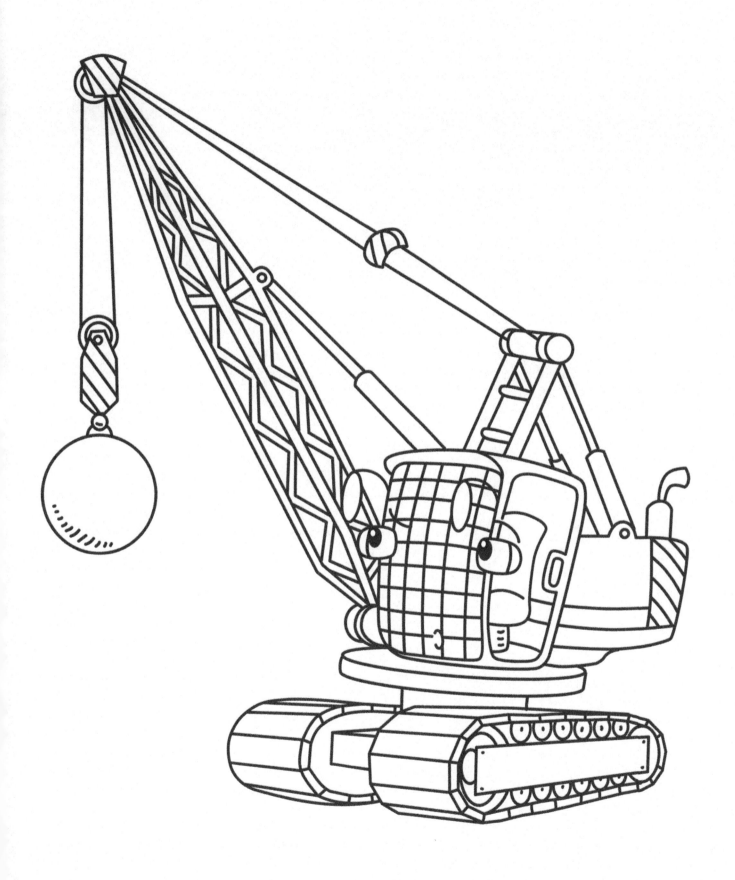

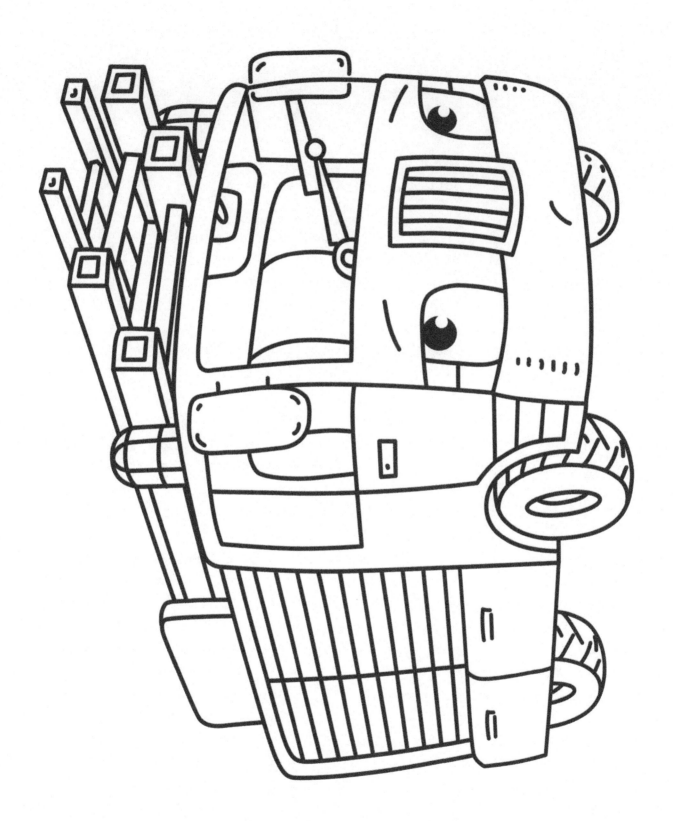

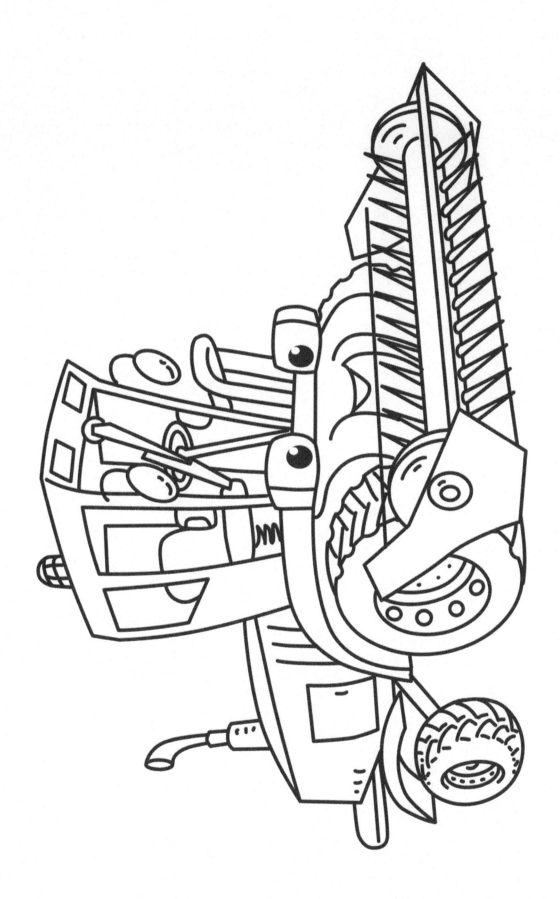

Matching Game

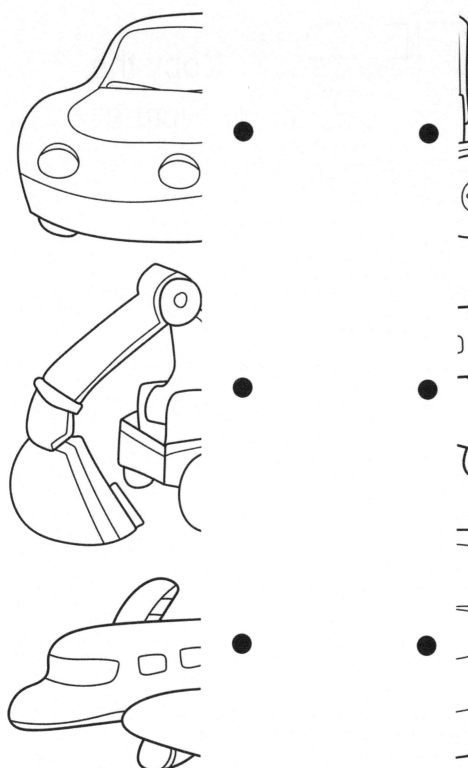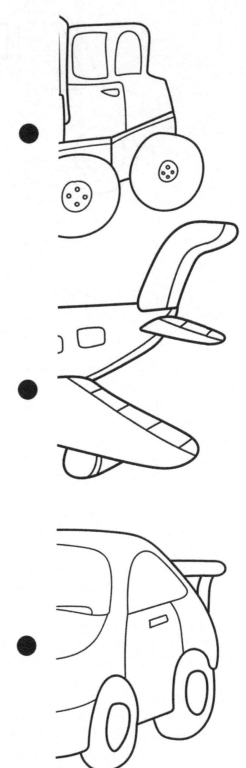

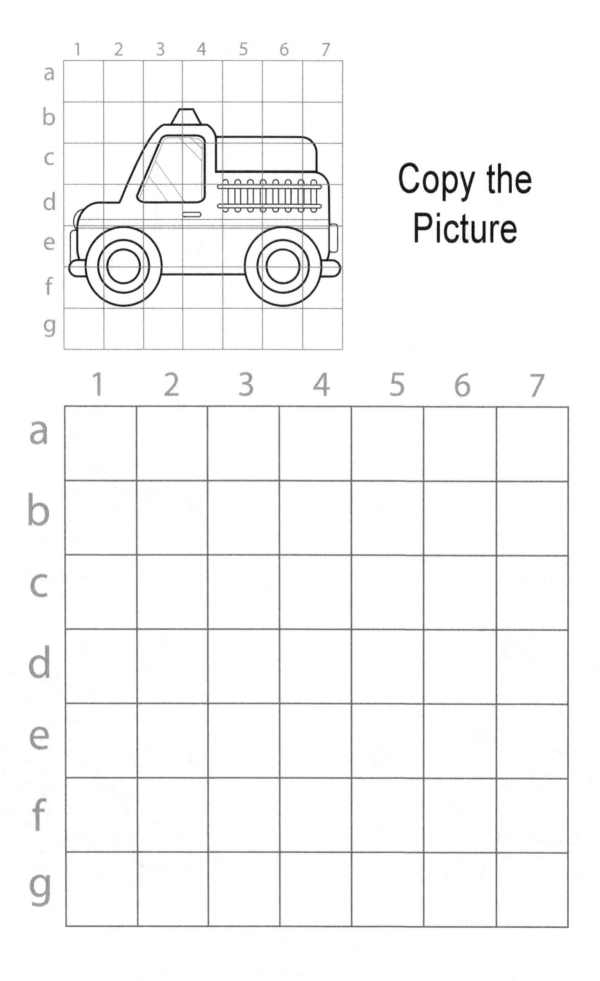

Copy the Picture

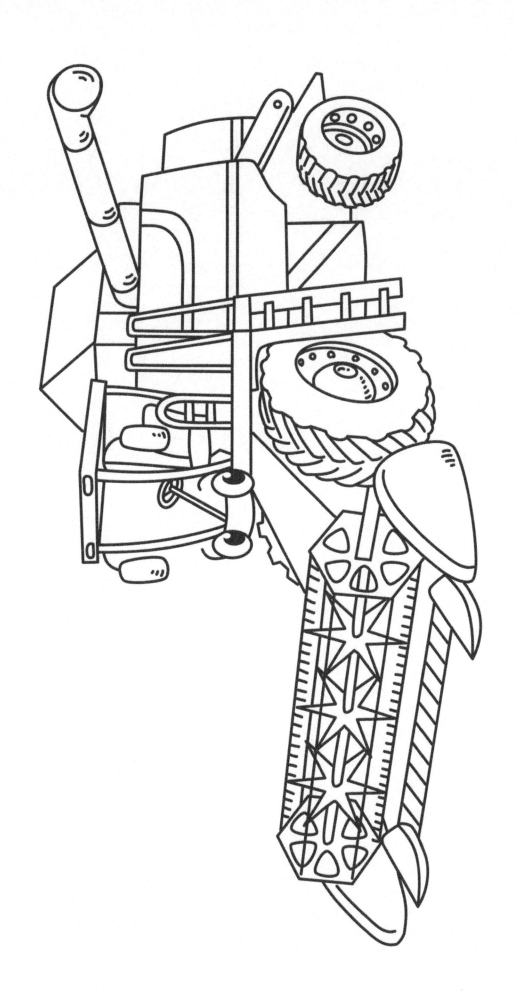

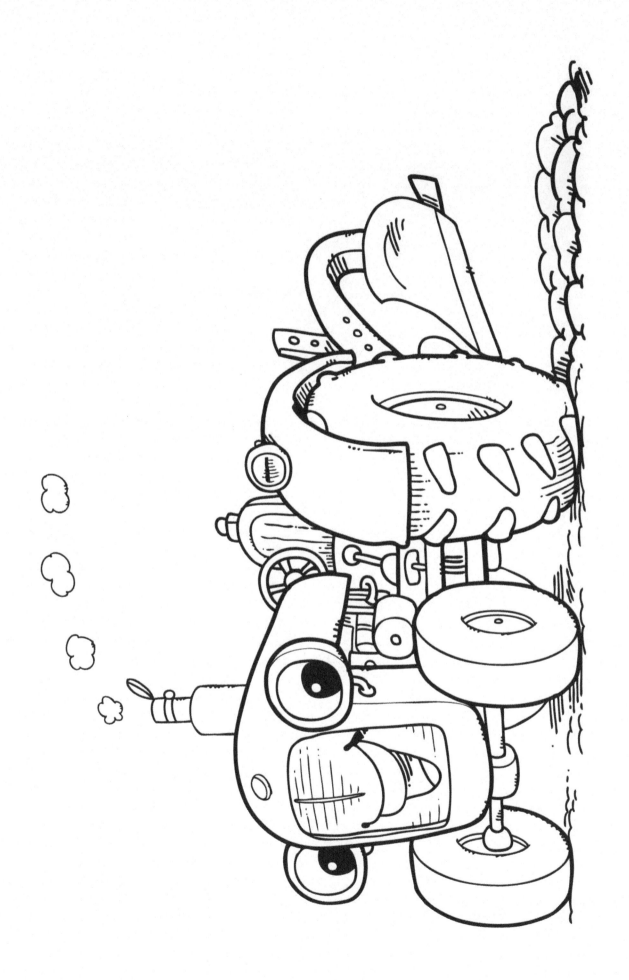

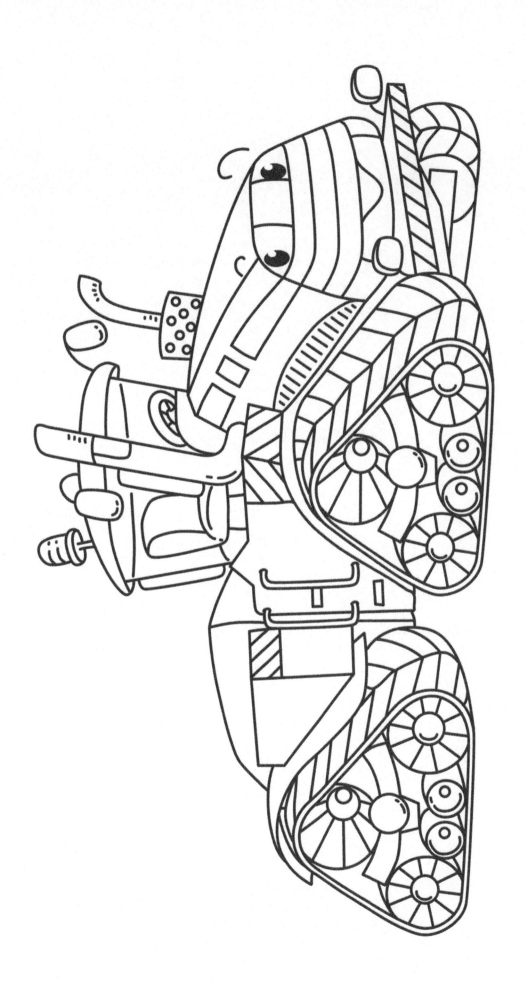

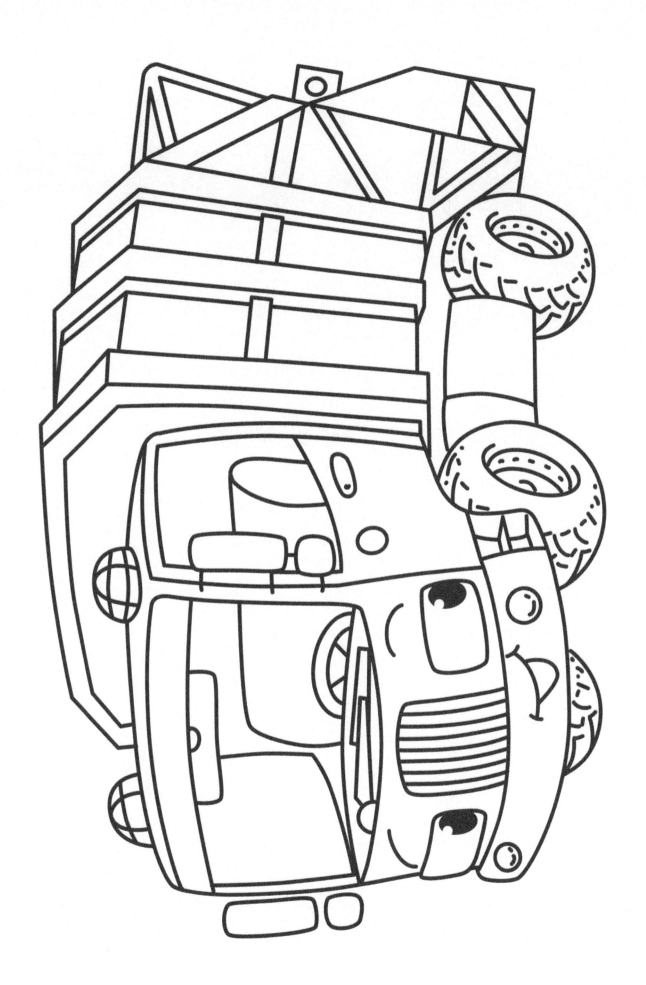

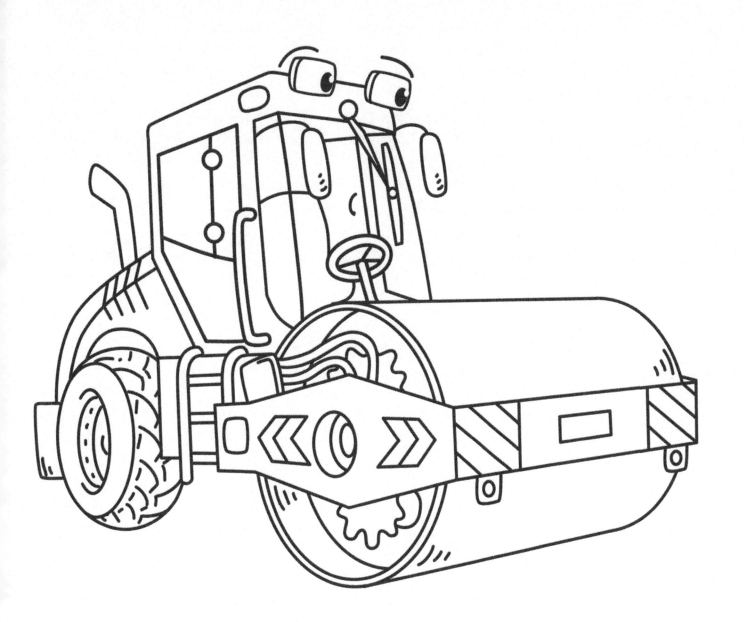

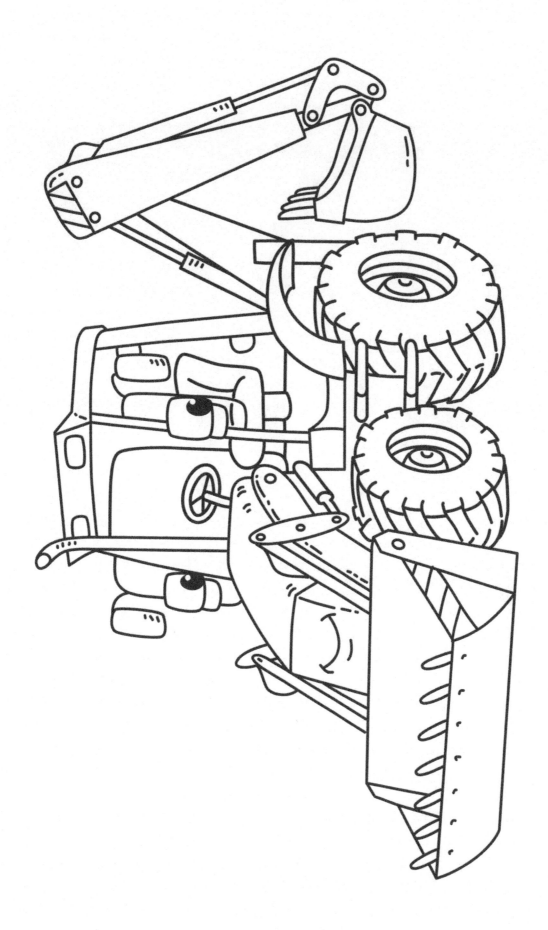

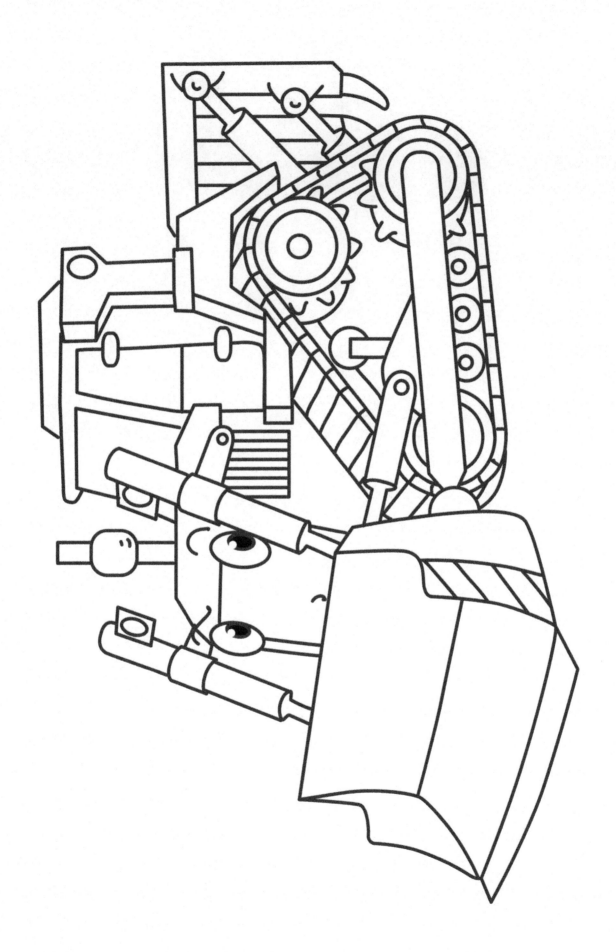

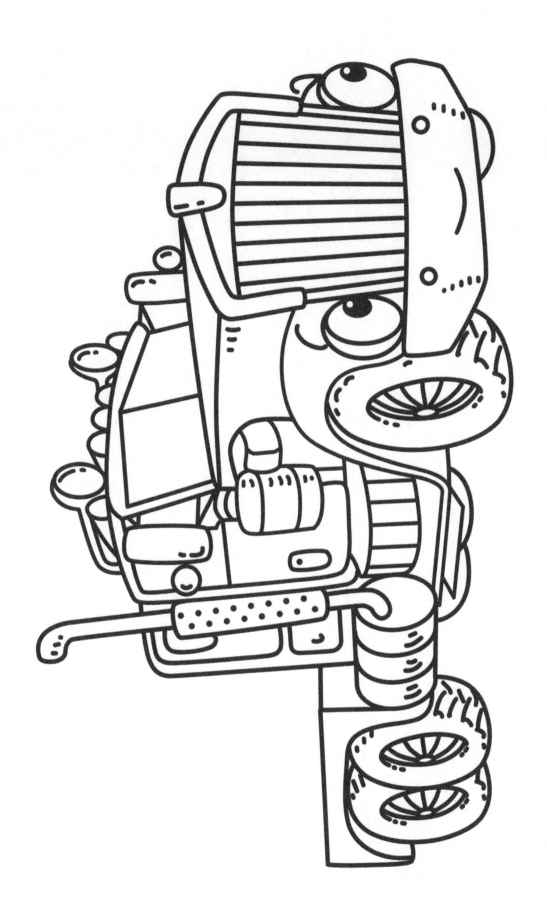

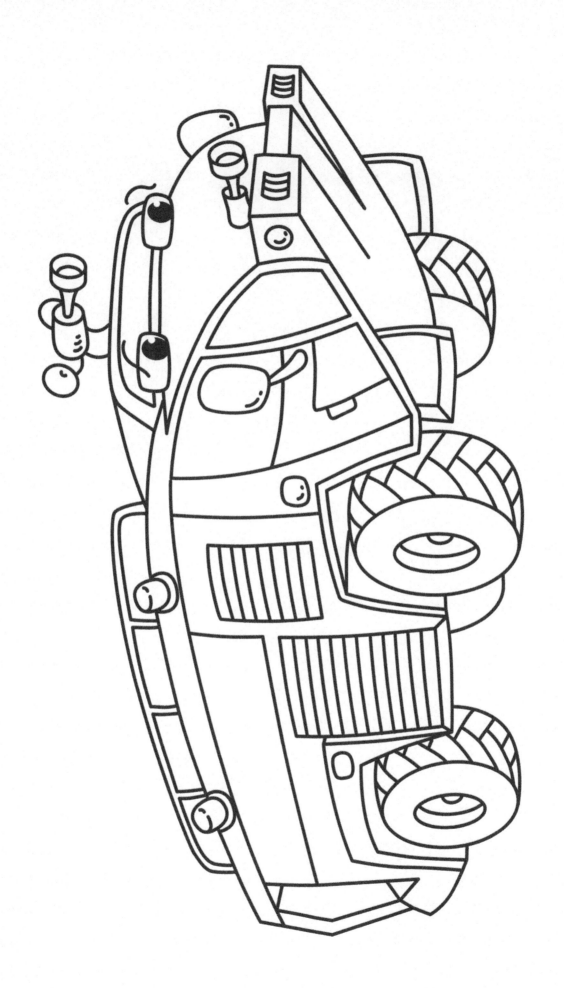

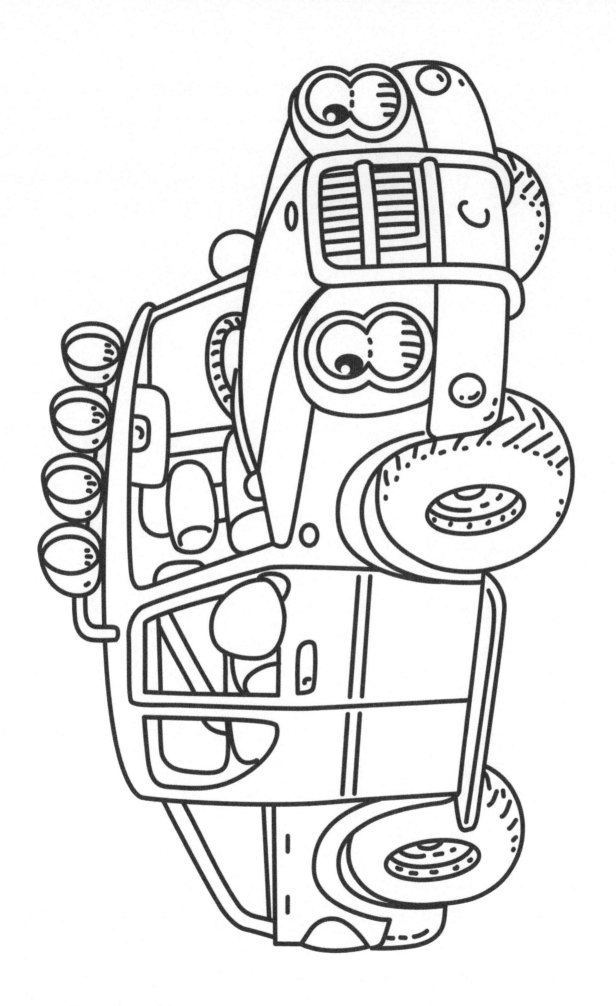

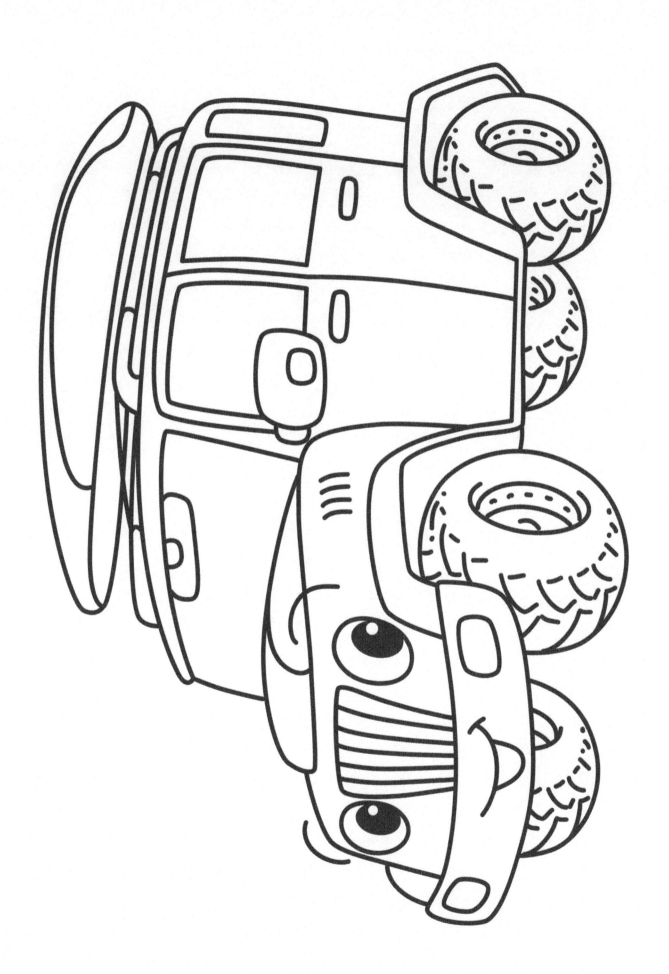

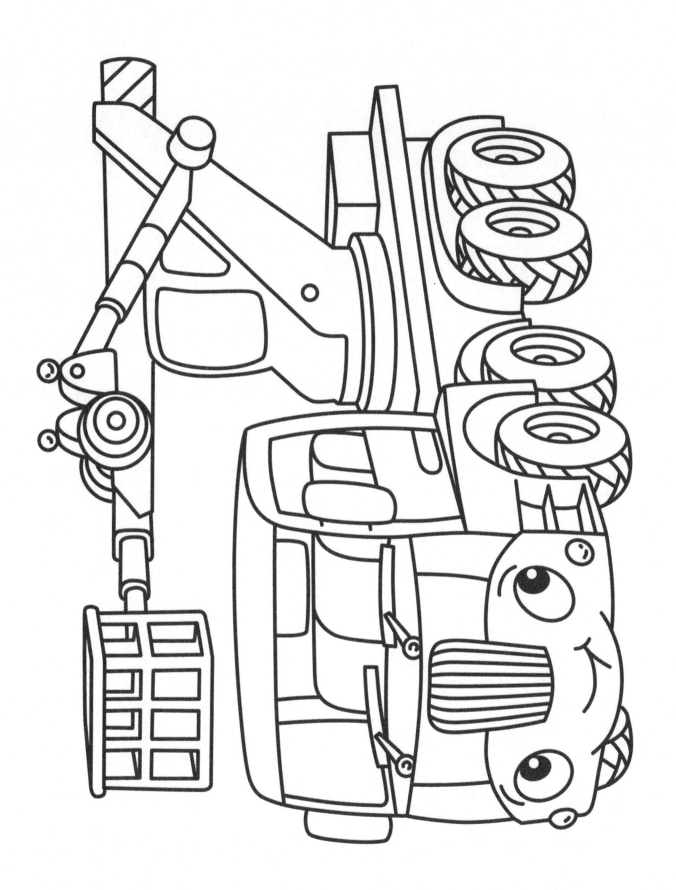

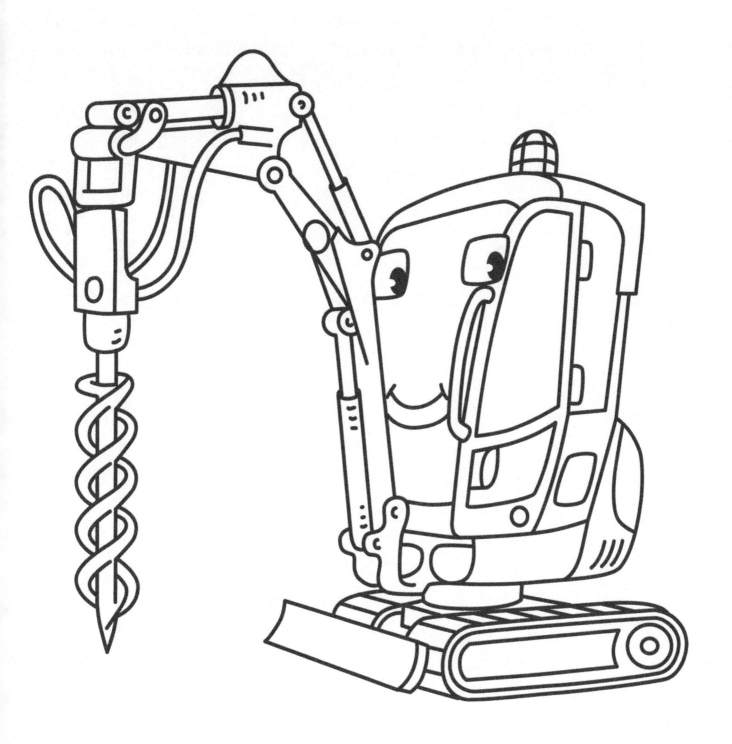

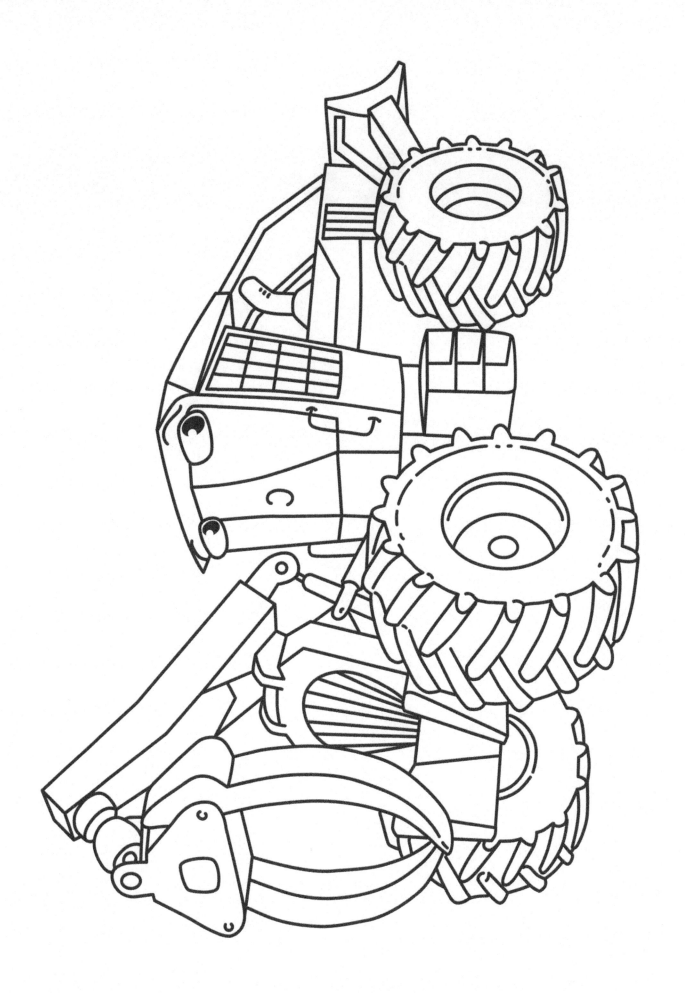

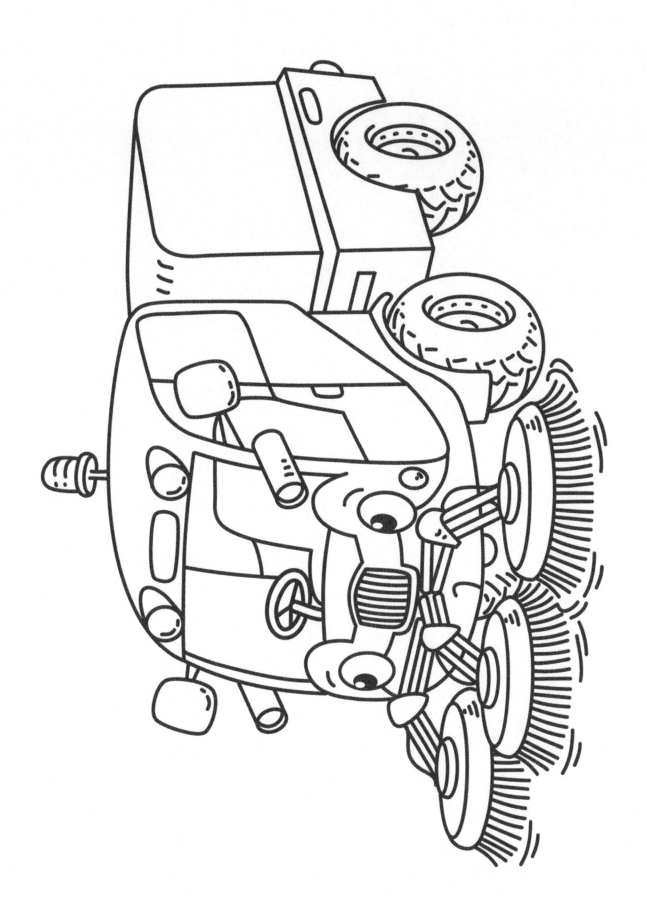

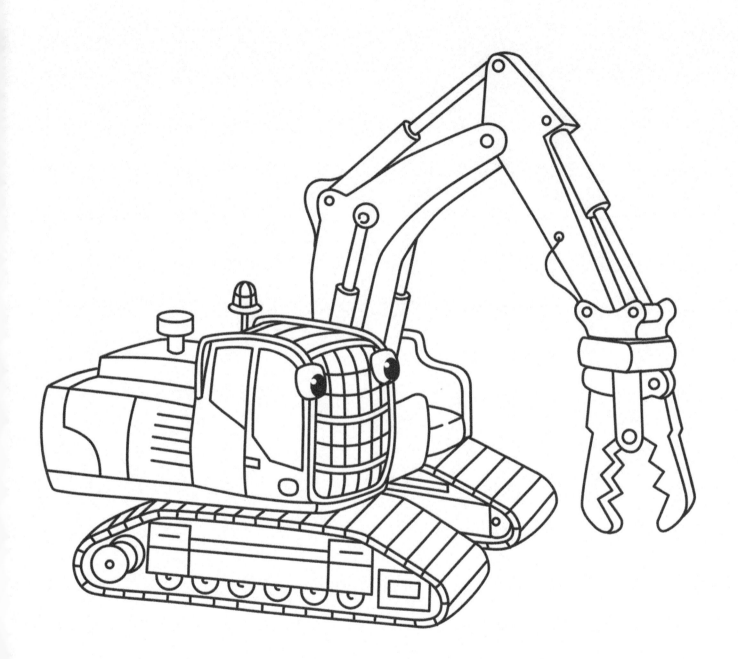

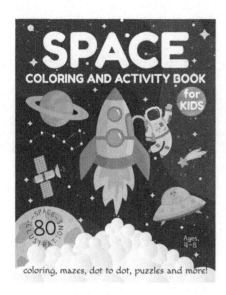

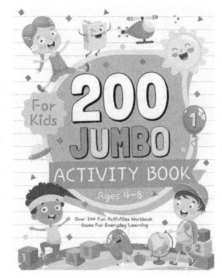

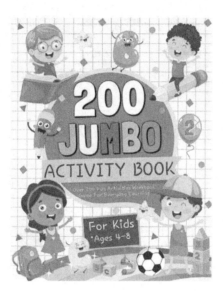

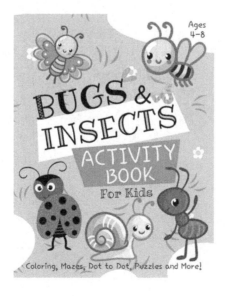

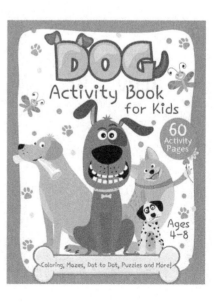

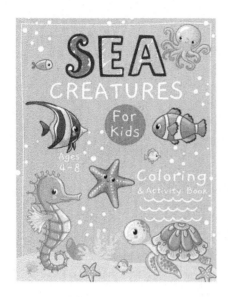

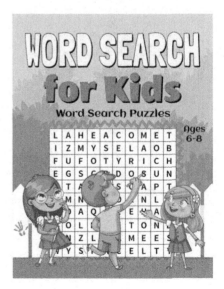

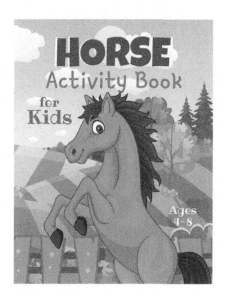

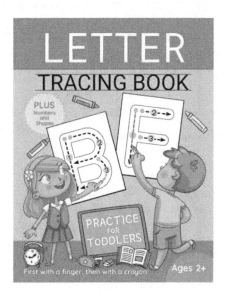

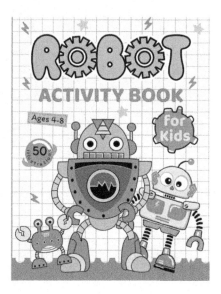

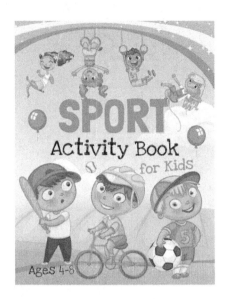

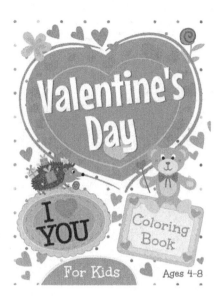

Made in United States
North Haven, CT
01 March 2023

33379643R00057